DACHSHUNDS
lightweights **littermates**

sharon montrose

Stewart, Tabori & Chang

New York

Published in 2005 by
Stewart, Tabori & Chang, 115 West 18th Street, New York, NY 10011
www.abramsbooks.com

Library of Congress Cataloging-in-Publication Data
Montrose, Sharon.
Dachshunds : lightweights-littermates / Sharon Montrose.
p. cm.
ISBN 1-58479-468-2
1. Dachshunds—Pictorial works. I. Title
SF429.D25M66 2005
636.753'8—dc22
2005042606

Designed by Sally Ann Field
Production by Alexis Mentor

The text of this book was composed in Eatwell Skinny & Eatwell Chubby by Chank Diesel.

Printed in China

10 9 8 7 6 5 4 3 2

Stewart, Tabori & Chang is a subsidiary of
LA MARTINIÈRE
GROUPE

lightweights **littermates** six weeks old

emme 2 lbs. 12 ozs.

moonie 2 lbs. 9 ozs.

reesa **2** lbs. 4 ozs.

lightweights **littermates** three weeks old

bo 1 lb. 4 ozs.

lin 1 lb. 3 ozs.

jiao 1 lb. 5 ozs.

lightweights **littermates** five weeks old

gerold **2** lbs. 4ozs.

maurice 2 lbs. 6 ozs.

tammy **2** lbs. **7** ozs.

lightweights **littermates** five weeks old

speck **1** lb. 3ozs.

mole **1**lb. *8*OZS.

djuna **1** lb. 5 OZS.

bing **1** lb. 5 ozs.

cola 1 lb. 6 ozs.

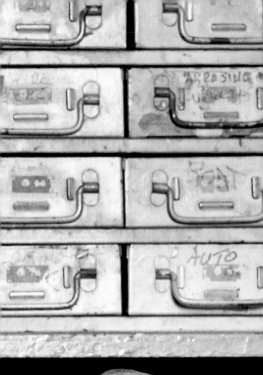

lightweights **littermates** seven weeks old

brian 2 lbs. 8 ozs.

earl 3 lbs. 6 ozs.

jeb 2 lbs. 11 ozs.

ophelia 2 lbs. 4 ozs.

flo **2** lbs. 6 ozs.

lightweights **littermates** four weeks old

brownie **2** lbs. 6ozs.

fozzy 2 lbs. 4 ozs.

beatrice **2** lbs. 4 ozs.

poke 2 lbs. 5 ozs.

lightweights **littermates** five weeks old

basie **1** lb. **6** ozs.

bird 1 lb. 8 ozs.

vaughn 1 lb. 7 ozs.

dexter 1 lb. 5 ozs.

ella 1 lb. 3 ozs.

mercer **1** lb.1oz.

lightweights littermates five weeks old

simon 2 lbs. 1 oz.

guinness 2 lbs. 5 ozs.

chap **2** lbs. **0** oz.

eva 2 lbs. 4 ozs.

lightweights **littermates** four weeks old

bouy 1 lb. 2 ozs.

leopold **1** lb.**4**ozs.

millie **1** lb. **3** ozs.

gretta 1 lb. 1 oz.

With many thanks to family and friends, as always.

Also, Hendrick and Sally.

Bob Weinberg.

My literary agent, Betsy Amster.

Leslie Stoker, Beth Huseman and the whole staff at Stewart, Tabori and Chang.

Everyone at the Icon.

Craig and everyone at Photo Center.

Charles Lee.

All the adorable little puppies and their breeder, Karen.

A very special thank you to Sally Ann Field.

And, especially, Spencer Starr.

Puppies Provided by: Stone Family Dachshunds 949-364-0336 www.stonesfamilydachshunds.com